JOKES FOR ADULTS

THE ULTIMATE ADULT ONLY JOKE BOOK

JENNY KELLETT

THE ULTIMATE ADULT ONLY JOKE BOOK

Copyright 2016 by Jenny Kellett, all rights reserved. Copyright and other intellectual property laws protect these materials. Reproduction or retransmission of the materials, in whole or in part, in any manner, without the prior written consent of the copyright holder, is a violation of copyright law.

ISBN-13: 978-1530070398
ISBN-10: 1530070392

I've just done my first autopsy, and according to the results the victim died of an autopsy.

ω

Next time you're feeling lonely, just remember that Forrest Gump got laid and he was retarded.

ω

Did you hear about the new and politically correct name for 'lesbian'?

It has been changed to 'vagitarian'.

I can't believe how many single girls in my area who want to meet me. Must be because of all the iPads I've won!

What did the sign on the front of the brothel say?

Beat it - we're closed.

Why did God give blondes 2% more brains than horses?

Because he didn't want them sh*tting in the streets during parades.

How did Burger King get Dairy Queen Pregnant?

He forgot to wrap his whopper.

ω

I swapped my sister's tampons with party poppers. Absolutely no sense of humor, that girl…

ω

What would happen if the Pilgrims had killed cats instead of turkeys?

We'd eat pussy every Thanksgiving.

Why did the blonde give up bowling for screwing?

The balls are lighter, and you don't have to change shoes.

ω

Yo mama is so fat I took a picture of her last Christmas and it's still printing.

ω

How is a penis like fishing?

The small ones you throw back, the medium ones you eat, the larger ones you mount.

How do you get four old ladies to shout 'f*ck!'?

Get a fifth old lady to shout 'Bingo'!

I remember when ADHD could be cured with a belt across the ass.

Why can't Miss Piggy count to 70?

Because she gets a frog in her throat at 69.

Top tip: Save money on expensive, name brand laxatives by buying a 99c Taco Bell burrito.

ω

Why don't bunnies make noise when they make love?

Because they have cotton balls.

ω

Never trust atoms, they make up everything.

What can a goose do, a duck can't, and a lawyer should?

Stick his bill up his ass.

Wait, so hallways in mental institutions aren't called psychopaths? Well, they should be…

Why do women rub their eyes when they get up in the morning?

They don't have balls to scratch.

ω

You're so hot, even my zipper is falling for you.

ω

They say the key to a long-lasting marriage is to marry your best friend. We're picking out a dress for Gary now.

In America we walk the dog, in China they wok the dog.

ω

Which sexual position produces the ugliest children?

Ask your mother.

ω

So we're attacking Syria because Syria attacked Syria.

I like my girl to be Hannah on the streets, but Miley in the sheets.

ω

"Don't judge a person by the way they look." - *Ugly People.*

ω

Friends are like trampolines. I've never had one, but they look fun.

How do you embarrass an archaeologist?

Give him a used tampon and ask him which period it came form.

ⓒⱽ

Who was the world's first carpenter?

Eve, because she made Adam's banana stand.

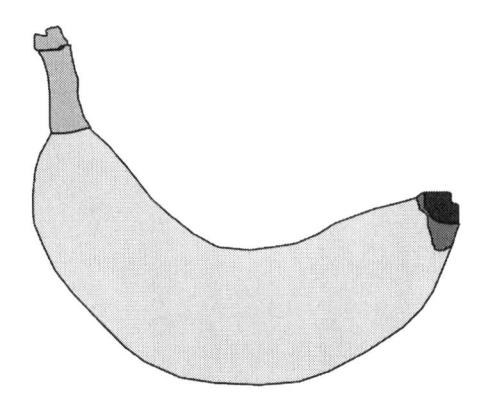

What gets easier to pick up the heavier it gets?

Women.

ω

You may have a hot body, but I have a hot bucket of chicken wings so who's the real winner here?

ω

You never know how picky you are until you're looking for porn.

Japanese Atheists don't believe in Godzilla.

ω

Why do hunters make the best lovers?

Because they go deep in the bush, shoot more than once and they eat what they shoot!

ω

If you're an astronaut and you don't end every relationship by saying 'Look, i just need space!', you're f*cking wasting everyone's time.

What did the letter O say to the letter Q?

Dude, your dick is hanging out.

ω

My wife treats me like God. She takes very little notice of my existence until she wants something.

ω

Yo mama is so fat she has more Chins than a Chinese phone book.

I no longer wish to be an adult. If anyone needs me, I'll be in my bed sheet and pillow fort… coloring.

ω

What did the blind man say when he was passing the fish market?

Good morning ladies!

ω

I don't need pepper spray to stop a mugger, I just open my wallet and blow the dust in their eyes.

They call themselves independent women until furniture needs to be moved.

ω

Everybody out there hates 'Crocs', but the company is worth over $2 billion? Some of you motherf*ckers are lying!

ω

Chuck Norris doesn't flush the toilet. He scares the shit out of it.

I'm not saying your girl is a ho… All I'm saying is she's easier than the corner piece in a puzzle.

My car has heated seats, and even a heated steering wheel, but only in summer.

Just gave my cat 7UP. She now has 16 lives.

What is the cheapest type of meat?

Deer balls, they're under a buck.

ω

I can't believe my girlfriend just called me old fashioned. And with her ankles showing, the slut.

ω

I understand how people feel when they see their ex with someone else. It's the same feeling I get when I see the pizza boy at my neighbor's house.

If she's learned her ABC's, it's time to teach her about the D.

ꙮ

How do you turn a dishwasher into a snowplough?

Give her a shovel.

ꙮ

If you've ever lost your phone, feel good in knowing that some mouse family somewhere now has a flat-screen TV.

What did the blonde's left leg say to her right leg?

Between the two of us, we can make a lot of money.

ω

Yo mama is so fat she got arrested at the airport for 10 pounds of crack.

Who can make more money in a week — a drug dealer or a prostitute?

The prostitute because she can wash and resell her crack.

Why is it called a Wonder Bra?

When she takes it off you wonder where her tits went.

What two words will clear out a men's changing room quicker than anything else?

Nice dick!

ω

What do women and police cars have in common?

They both make a lot of noise to let you know they're coming.

If sex is a pain in the butt, you're doing it wrong!

What do horny women order at Subway?

Footlongs!

How do you make five pounds of fat look good?

Put a nipple on it.

My girlfriend dumped me and gave the reason that I'm the 'King of Stupid Comparisons'. I feel like a bacon sandwich on chemotherapy.

ω

Why are condoms transparent?

So that sperm can at least enjoy the scenery, even if their entry is restricted!

ω

I asked Santa for something to wear and something to play with. He left me a pair of trousers with a hole in the pocket.

Why do you never see a chicken in underwear?

Because their peckers are on their face.

ω

How does the blonde turn on the light after she has had sex?

She opens the car door.

ω

Grammar is the difference between 'I helped my Uncle Jack, off a horse', and 'I helped my uncle jack off a horse'.

Why does a bride smile when she walks up the aisle?

She knows she's given her last blow job.

ω

What did one saggy boob say to the other saggy boob?

If we don't get some support soon, people are going to think we're nuts.

ω

I think it's going to take a joint effort to completely legalize marijuana.

Don't hold your farts in, because then they travel up your spine to your brain - and that's how shitty ideas are invented.

ꌗ

What did the hurricane say to the coconut tree?

Hold onto your nuts - this is no ordinary blow job!

Why is reading Playboy like reading National Geographic?

You get to see many great places you'll never get to visit.

ω

If it really is the thought that counts, I should be in prison.

ω

What did Cinderella do when she got to the ball?

Gagged.

Cosmopolitan magazine says there are 21 ways to arouse your man. I'm pretty sure all you have to do is touch my dick.

ω

Why was Philip's girlfriend disappointed?

Because she found out that Philip's 24 inch was a TV.

What's the speed limit of sex?

68, because at 69 you have to turn around.

ω

How does a man show that he is planning for the future?

He buys two cases of beer instead of one.

ω

What do you call a gay dinosaur?

Mega-sore-ass.

What does a Chinese man call his pet lion?

Ryan.

What's the ultimate rejection?

When you're masturbating and your hand falls asleep.

I realized I probably wasn't the best listener when my friend had to come out to me twice.

ω

My girlfriend asked me if I was high, I just laughed. Uncontrollably. For 15 minutes.

ω

Why is air like sex?

Because it's no big deal unless you're not getting any.

My bed wasn't feeling well this morning so I stayed home to take care of it.

ω

I lost a very good friend and drinking partner yesterday…. his finger got caught in a wedding ring.

ω

What do you call it when a 90 year old man masturbates successfully?

Miracle whip.

Why do men find it difficult to make eye contact?

Breasts don't have eyes.

ꇴ

What do a Rubix cube and a penis have in common?

The longer you play with them, the harder they get.

What's black and fuzzy and hangs from the ceiling?

A blonde electrician.

ω

My doctor was checking my balls for lumps the other day. It got awkward when I ran my fingers through his hair.

ω

What do a clitoris, an anniversary, an a toilet have in common?

Men always miss them.

What happens the smog lifts over Los Angeles?

UCLA.

ⓒⓒ

I went on the internet to check the weather. That was 12 years ago.

ⓒⓒ

What do you call a country where everyone is pissed?

A urination.

What are three two-letter words that mean small?

'Is it in'.

Did you hear about the Mexican train killer?

He had locomotives.

What do you call a cheap circumcision?

A rip off!

The word of the day is legs. Spread the word!

ω

How is a man like a snowstorm?

You never know when he's coming, how many inches you'll get, or how long it will last.

ω

I went out on a limb today and I'm still stuck in the tree.

Twerking and selfie have been added to the dictionary. Future and optimism have been taken out.

ω

Why did the sperm cross the road?

Because I put on the wrong socks before I went for a walk.

ω

What's worse than spiders on your piano?

Crabs on your organ.

Farts are just ghosts of the things we eat.

ω

Best mind-f*ck pick-up line: 'If I asked you to have sex with me, would your answer be the same as the answer to this question?'

ω

How do you kill a circus clown?

Kick him in the juggler.

What do electric trains and breasts have in common?

They're intended for children, but it's the men that end up playing with them.

ω

What's six inches long, two inches wide, and drives women wild?

Money.

What do a pizza delivery man and a gynecologist have in common?

They can both smell it but they can't touch it.

ᶜ³ᵒ

What's slimy, long and smells of pork?

Kermit the frog's finger.

What's the difference between you and eggs?

Eggs get laid and you don't.

Ꙃ

Why does a penis have a hole in the end?

So men can be open-minded.

Why was Newton shocked when he saw a beautiful girl naked?

He found his d*ck going up, which was against his Law of Gravity.

ω

Why does the law society prohibit sex between lawyers and their clients?

To prevent clients from being billed twice for essentially the same service.

What has 75 balls and screws old ladies?

Bingo!

ω

Diarrhea is hereditary. It runs in your jeans.

ω

A penis is the lightest thing in the world. Even a thought can lift it!

How do you find a blind man in a nudist colony? It's not hard.

ω

How many newspapers can a woman hold between her legs?

One Post, Two Globes, and many Times.

ω

What is the definition of a menstrual period?

A bloody waste of f*cking time.

Sign outside a prostitute's house: Married men are NOT allowed. We serve the needy, not the greedy.

ω

What's the last thing that Tickle Me Elmo receives before he leaves the factory?

Two test tickles.

Which is the smallest hotel in the world?

Vagina Inn. It can accommodate only one standing guest with his luggage hanging outside.

ᗢ

What do you find in a clean nose?

Fingerprints.

Why did the blonde make love in the microwave?

She wanted to have a baby in 9 minutes.

ω

How do we know when men invented maps?

Who else would turn an inch into a mile!

ω

Yo mama is so fat, not even Dora can explore her.

Why are men like cars?

Because they always pull out before they check to see if anyone else is coming.

ω

Viagra now available in eye drops; you don't get an erection but you look hard.

ω

What did the boy vampire say to the girl vampire?

See you next period.

What did the egg say to the boiling water?

How can you expect me to get hard so fast - I only just got laid!

ω

What does bungee jumping and hookers have in common?

They both cost 100 bucks and if the rubber breaks, you're screwed.

Why do dwarfs laugh when they run?

Because the grass tickles their balls.

ω

Yo mama so ugly her birth certificate is an apology letter from the condom factory.

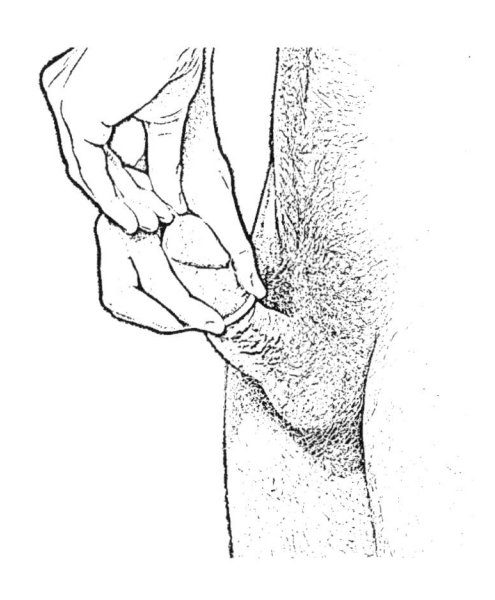

Why did Sally fall out of the tree?

Because she had no arms.

Knock knock.

Who's there?

Not Sally.

ω

Why does a squirrel swim on its back?

To keep its nuts dry.

How can you tell a sumo wrestler from a feminist?

A sumo wrestler shaves his legs.

ω

How many animals can you get into a pair of tights?

10 little piggies, 2 calves, 1 beaver, 1 ass, 1 pussy, thousands of hares and a dead fish no one can ever find.

Killing for peace is like f*cking for virginity.

ω

What did Adam say to Eve?

Stand back, I don't know how big this thing gets!

ω

Why is sex similar to shaving?

No matter how well you do it today, tomorrow you have to do it again.

What do you call an open can of tuna in a lesbian's apartment?

Potpourri.

ꓖꓳ

Why do blonde's get confused in the ladies room?

They have to pull their own pants down.

What do a dildo and soybeans have in common?

They're both meat substitutes.

What did Bill Clinton say to Monica?

I told you to lick my erection, not ruin my election.

I named my hard drive 'dat ass' so that once a month my computer asks if I want to 'back dat ass up'.

Why is it good for boys to read Playboy magazine?

It improves hand-eye coordination.

ω

I hate it when I'm about to hug someone really sexy and my face hits the mirror.

ω

What should you do if you girlfriend starts smoking?

Slow down and use some lubricant.

What do blondes and the Bermuda triangle have in common?

They have both swallowed a lot of semen.

ω

How are women and tornadoes alike?

They both moan like hell when they come, and take the house when they leave.

ω

Why did the snowman smile?

Because the snowblower was coming.

What's the difference between your job and a dead prostitute?

Your job still sucks!

ω

When do you kick a dwarf in the balls?

When he's standing next to your girlfriend saying her hair smells nice.

ω

What's long and hard and has cum in it?

A cucumber.

Why can't you play Uno with a Mexican?

They steal all the green cards.

ꊛ

Did you hear about the guy who died of a Viagra overdose?

They couldn't close his casket.

ꊛ

What do you call 2 guys fighting over a slut?

Tug-of-whore.

What's the difference between a bowling ball and a blonde?

You can only fit three fingers inside a bowling ball!

Why was the guitar teacher arrested?

For fingering A minor.

What do the Mafia and a pussy have in common?

One slip of the tongue, and you're in deep shit.

ω

Why do men get their great ideas in bed?

Because they're plugged into a genius!

A daughter asked her mother how to spell penis, her mom said you should have asked me last night, it was on the tip of my tongue.

ω

What has got two legs and bleeds?

Half a dog!

ω

What is the difference between an illegal immigrant and E.T.?

E.T. eventually went home!

What's the difference between being hungry and horny?

Where you put the cucumber.

What kind of bees produce milk?

Boo-bees.

What do you call a lesbian dinosaur?

A lickalotapis.

Why did Tigger look in the toilet?

Because he was looking for Pooh.

ω

Do you know what the square root of 69 is?

8 something.

But do you know what 6.9 is?

A good thing screwed up by a period.

What did the banana say to the vibrator?

Why are YOU shaking? She's going to eat me.

ω

One day, a little boy wrote to Santa Claus, 'Please send me a sister.' Santa Claus wrote him back, 'Ok, send me your mother.'

What does a 75 year old woman have between her breasts that a 25 year old doesn't?

Her navel.

ω

What does a good bar and a good woman have in common?

Liquor in the front and poker in the back!

Why does the Easter Bunny hide Easter eggs?

He doesn't want anyone knowing he's been f*cking the chickens!

ω

What is the difference between erotic and kinky?

Erotic is using a feather....kinky is using the whole chicken.

Why doesn't Mexico have an Olympic team?

Because everybody who can run, jump and swim are already in the U.S.

ω

What do u call a bunny with a bent dick?

F*cks Funny.

What's black, white, and red all over and doesn't fit through a revolving door?

A nun with a spear through her head.

ω

Did you hear about the Chinese couple that had a dyslexic baby?

They named him Sum Ting Wong.

ω

Why don't they have any toilet paper in KFC?

Because its finger licking good!

Why did the girl fall off the swing?

Because she had no arms.

ɞ

What's thirty feet long and smells like urine?

Line dancing at a nursing home.

ɞ

How do you get a fat woman into bed?

Piece of cake!

And that's all, folks!

Thanks again for purchasing this book — it was incredibly fun to put together.

If you loved it as much as we do — please leave us a review on Amazon, it allows us to keep producing bigger, better and dirtier books!